1315

920
STO

Stone, Melissa

Larger than life

$14.64

DATE			
SEP 25 1997			
OCT 02 1992			
NOV 18 1992			
MAR 28 1998			

Larger Than Life

Program Consultants

Stephanie Abraham Hirsh, Ph.D.
Associate Director
National Staff Development Council
Dallas, Texas

Louise Matteoni, Ph.D.
Professor of Education
Brooklyn College
City University of New York

Karen Tindel Wiggins
Social Studies Consultant
Richardson Independent School District
Richardson, Texas

Renee Levitt
Educational Consultant
Scarsdale, New York

Steck-Vaughn Company

A Subsidiary of National Education Corporation

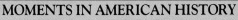

MOMENTS IN AMERICAN HISTORY

Larger Than Life

BY
Melissa Stone

Steck-Vaughn Literature Library
Moments in American History

RISKING IT ALL
REBELLION'S SONG
CREATIVE DAYS
RACING TO THE WEST
YOU DON'T OWN ME!
CLOUDS OF WAR
A CRY FOR ACTION
LARGER THAN LIFE
FLYING HIGH
BRIGHTER TOMORROWS

Illustrations: Brian Pinkney: pp. 8-9, 10, 12, 14-15, 17, 19; Christa Kieffer: pp. 20-21, 23, 24, 26-27, 28-29, 31; Steve Cieslawski: cover art, pp. 32-33, 34, 37, 38, 40, 43; Lyle Miller: pp. 44-45, 46, 49, 51, 52-53, 55; Rae Ecklund: pp. 56-57, 59, 61, 62, 65, 67; Al Fiorentino pp. 68-69, 71, 73, 74, 77, 79.

Project Editor: Anne Souby

Design: Kirchoff/Wohlberg, Inc.

ISBN 0-8114-4082-6 (pbk.)
ISBN 0-8114-2672-6 (lib. bdg.)   LC 89-110894

CONTENTS

CARRIE CHAPMAN CATT ➤
Her quiet dedication
finally won women the
right to vote.
(1872-1920)

◄ JACK JOHNSON
From the docks to the
boxing ring, he was a
self-made champion.
(1893-1910)

ALVIN YORK ➤
Behind the battle medals
and decorations was a man
of principle and action.
(1917-1918)

1920

BILLY MITCHELL ➤
In the development of
air power, he was ahead
of his time.
(1920-1936)

◄ **LANGSTON HUGHES**
He expressed the dignity
and spirit of his people
through poetry.
(1920-1926)

RUDOLPH VALENTINO ➤
Without saying a word,
this star of the silver
screen made fans swoon.
(1921-1926)

JACK JOHNSON
WORLD HEAVYWEIGHT
CHAMPION

Well, Jack, you seem to have a talent for boxing. You'll have to train long and hard, but if you keep coming to the gym and working out, who knows? The world may yet sit up and take notice of you. You may have a future in boxing after all.

J ACK Johnson let out a sigh of relief as a loud whistle signaled the end of work. Today, March 1, 1893, had been his first day on the docks. After ten long hours of lifting crates and loading ships, he was exhausted.

As he gathered his belongings, an eerie darkness settled over the harbor. Johnson suddenly felt nervous. He knew the waterfront was a dangerous part of town, especially for a fifteen-year-old black boy.

He headed up the alley toward the center of Galveston, Texas, where he lived. After walking a short distance, he noticed a big, burly man coming toward him. Johnson bent his head and kept walking.

"Hey, you! What are you doing here? This isn't your part of town. We don't like your kind around here. I'll have to teach you a lesson." The man pushed the petrified boy against the brick wall and punched him hard in the ribs. Johnson fell to the ground, gasping for breath.

"Don't let me catch you here again, or I'll really show you something," the man threatened.

Johnson felt his blood boil. It was his first taste of real prejudice.

"It's not fair," he thought angrily. "I have just as much right to be here as he does. Someday, I'm going to get even. Nobody's going to pick on me again."

The next day, Johnson visited a local gym.

"I want to learn how to box," he told the trainer.

"Why?" the trainer asked, looking at Johnson's tall, skinny frame. "You don't look like a boxer to me."

"I want to be able to protect myself. If someone picks on me, I want to be able to fight back."

Johnson found that he had a natural talent for boxing. He was fast on his feet and had quick, graceful moves. He could anticipate what his opponents were going to do. Best of all, he could strike a sharp blow with either hand. His left hook was as strong as his right punch.

"You keep training," the gym owner told him, "and you could go far in boxing. You might even become a professional fighter."

Johnson decided he *would* keep at it. He had found something he could do well. Every morning before going down to the docks to work, he stopped in at the gym. He lifted weights, jumped rope, and ran laps. Gradually, he built up his strength. As his pride and confidence grew, he walked about the waterfront fearlessly. He could protect himself against any aggressor.

I N 1899, Jack Johnson decided to give up his work as a longshoreman.

"I'm tired of this kind of work," he told his

brother Cal. "There's no future for me here. I'm going to become a professional boxer. I'm good. I think I can make it to the top."

"Jack, are you crazy? There are no black men in professional boxing. You won't be accepted. No one will fight you. You'll end up traveling from town to town with a group of black exhibition fighters. Is that really what you want?"

"No," said Johnson firmly. "I can do better than that. I intend to fight the people who hold the titles. I intend to be the heavyweight boxing champion."

At first Johnson had no luck breaking boxing's color barrier. Unable to get any fights with professional boxers, he joined a black exhibition group. It looked as though Cal's prediction had come true. Johnson, however, refused to settle for a life of exhibition matches and small-time fights.

Boldly Johnson contacted some of the top black fighters in the country. In just three years he won most of his fights and earned a reputation as one of the best black fighters of the day.

"Now," thought Johnson, "I'm going to break into the ranks of professional boxing."

Johnson's first big fight against a professional came in 1902. George Gardner, a highly regarded light-heavyweight, agreed to fight him.

"I'm the best," boasted Gardner. "I can beat anyone, and I can beat this upstart with one hand tied behind my back."

Johnson trained fiercely for the fight. He knew this was his chance to prove that he could become a champion.

On the night of the fight, Johnson was in perfect form. He beat Gardner without much trouble at all. Johnson had taken the first big step in his plan. He was on his way to the top.

ONE by one Johnson picked off the top contenders for the world heavyweight boxing title. At last he had beaten them all. The only opponent left was Tommy Burns, the reigning world champion. It was time to fulfill his dream. It was time to become the heavyweight champion of the world.

On December 26, 1908, Johnson climbed into the ring with Burns. By this time, Johnson had developed his own unique style. He entered the arena with a look of confidence, smiling and waving to the crowd. He pretended that he heard no boos from the audience.

When the first round began, Johnson appeared to be dancing as he bounced around the ring. Again and again Burns swiped at Johnson, but Johnson proved too quick for him. Burns's fists hit nothing but air. When Johnson caught Burns off guard in the fourteenth round, he easily knocked him out. It had been a long fight, but Johnson had won.

"I've done it! I've done it!" he shouted victoriously as he returned to his dressing room. "I'm the first black man ever to win the title! I'm the new world heavyweight champ!"

The boxing fans, however, did not share Johnson's happiness. They could not accept him as the heavyweight champion. They could not believe that a black man was the world's best boxer. Around the country cries went up to dethrone the new champ.

"Someone must wipe the golden smile from Jack Johnson's face!" declared one of his critics.

Several boxers were anxious to meet Johnson in the ring so they could defeat him. Each one claimed to be the "Great White Hope." And each one took his turn against Johnson. But they all went down in defeat. At last the boxing managers turned to a retired champ for help.

JIM Jeffries had reigned as heavyweight champ for six years. He had retired undefeated in 1905. But by 1909, at the age of 35, he didn't look like a boxer. He weighed more than 300 pounds. Jeffries didn't really want to come out of retirement. But with so many people pressuring him, he finally conceded. He agreed to fight Jack Johnson in what was billed as "The Fight of the Century."

Jeffries spent a year in rugged training. He ran. He skipped rope. He dieted. He coaxed his body back into fighting shape.

At last the day of the fight drew near. Johnson knew that many fans wanted to see him lose. Still, he stayed calm. He had come a long way since his days as an angry young man on the Galveston docks. He had stuck to his plan. He had proven his worth, if not to the public, at least to himself.

By midday of July 4, 1910, over 16,000 fans had crammed into the arena in Reno, Nevada. The heat in the stadium was suffocating. Johnson stood waiting for the fight. Sweat ran down his face and body.

"Well," thought Johnson, "this is the final test. If I can beat Jeffries, people will have to admit I'm the best in the world."

WHEN the bell sounded for the start of round one, Johnson saw Jeffries rushing at him from across the ring.

"He's going for the quick knockout," thought Johnson, ducking to avoid the punch.

As Johnson turned around, Jeffries lunged at him again. Jeffries, who outweighed Johnson by over twenty pounds, was trying to use his weight to pin Johnson against the ropes. Johnson, however, was too fast on his feet. He moved easily from one side of the ring to the other. He never gave Jeffries the chance to hit him.

The second round went much the same as the first. Jeffries swung desperately at Johnson. But he couldn't make any direct hits. Then, in the third round, Johnson began his attack. Jeffries staggered as he was caught by a sharp left jab. That punch stunned the crowd. Johnson also began to flash his famous, confident smile.

"Come on now, Mr. Jeff," he teased. "Let me see what you've got. Do something, man."

But there was nothing Jeffries could do against Johnson. By the seventh round, everyone could see that Jeffries stood no chance. His face was swollen. His right eye was closing. The power had vanished from his punches. By the fourteenth round, he could hardly defend himself.

In the fifteenth round, Johnson knocked him halfway out of the ring. Somehow Jeffries managed to get back on his feet. Johnson knocked him down again. At that point, Jeffries' manager threw the towel into the ring to signal defeat. Jack Johnson had won the fight!

As Johnson walked triumphantly out of the arena, he flashed his golden smile at the crowd. His dream had come true. Jack Johnson had shown that he was truly the heavyweight boxing champion of the world.

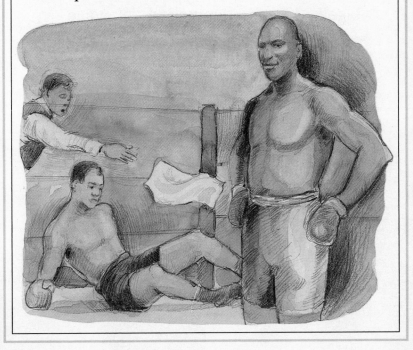

CARRIE CHAPMAN CATT

ORGANIZER FOR SUFFRAGE

Women have been trying to win the right to vote ever since the United States was founded. As far back as the American Revolution, women like Abigail Adams demanded a voice in government. We have been ignored long enough! It has been a long, slow process. But maybe the time has come at last!

E VERYONE was talking about it. With only a week to go, the 1872 Presidential election had completely captured the public's attention. Carrie Lane was only thirteen years old, but she was excited about the election. She felt proud when her father discussed the issues with her.

When Election Day finally arrived, Carrie jumped out of bed and ran down the narrow staircase to the kitchen. Her mother was cooking breakfast, and the smell of sausage filled the air.

"Today's the day, right, Mother?" she asked.

"What day?" asked Mrs. Lane, dropping another sausage into the pan.

"The day you and Father go into town to vote!" Carrie exclaimed.

Her mother laughed. "Carrie, you have the strangest ideas." She put a plate of eggs on the table. "Only men can vote. Women have never been allowed to vote. I'm sure we never will be."

Carrie felt deeply disappointed. "That means when I'm older, I won't be able to vote, either," she said. "That isn't fair! I'm as smart as any boy in my class. My ideas are just as good. Why shouldn't girls be able to vote?"

"Now, Carrie," said her mother, "it's silly to fret about it. Sit down and eat your breakfast."

Carrie sat down to breakfast, but she couldn't

stop thinking about it. "When I'm older," she vowed, "I'm going to change things. Someday I will vote in an election."

Carrie was a good student. She decided that after she finished high school, she wanted to go to college. But when she told her parents, they didn't agree.

"Why on earth do you want to go to college?" her mother asked. "You don't need an education to be a wife and mother!"

"Besides," said her father, "college is very expensive."

"I'll pay my own way," said Carrie.

After she graduated from high school, Carrie took a job as a teacher. She saved every penny she could. In 1877, she had enough money to enroll in Iowa State University. Every day after her classes, she worked washing dishes. Then she studied far into the night.

"I'm very tired," she wrote her family. "Still, it's worth it. I'm learning so much!"

After Carrie finished her degree in 1880, she was offered the position of high school principal in Mason City, Iowa.

Carrie couldn't believe it. "A woman principal!" she thought. "I'm sure I can do the job. I will go to Mason City!"

Two years later, Carrie was promoted to superintendent of schools. Carrie was the first woman to hold this position in Iowa.

AT the age of 26, Carrie met a young man named Leo Chapman. In a few months, they got married. The following year, they decided to move to San Francisco. Leo wanted to buy a newspaper there. Soon after arriving, Leo caught typhoid fever and died.

Carrie was numb with grief. Her life seemed aimless. She was alone and confused. One day, as Carrie wrote a letter to her family back in Iowa, she was struck by a vivid memory. She remembered sitting in the farmhouse watching her mother cook breakfast. She could almost hear her mother saying, "Women have never been allowed to vote. I'm sure we never will be." And she remembered her own pledge to change things.

"Now is the time to keep my promise," she thought as she sealed the letter. "I will go back to Iowa and join the suffrage movement. I will devote my life to helping women get the vote."

In Iowa, Carrie began to organize new suffrage clubs throughout the state. Then she organized a regional conference. Susan B. Anthony, the famous president of the National Woman Suffrage Association, was one of the speakers.

The conference ran very smoothly. Carrie's ability impressed Miss Anthony. The 72-year-old leader complimented Carrie on her efficiency.

"I need an enthusiastic young woman to travel with me and set up speaking engagements," Miss Anthony said. "I think your talent and energy can give the movement a real boost."

Carrie traveled all over the country with "Aunt Susan" and other suffrage leaders. Carrie's bright, forceful personality attracted people to her. Everyone listened to what she had to say.

In 1890, Carrie received her second proposal of marriage, from a man named George Catt.

"I like you very much, George," said Carrie. "But I can't get married. I mustn't give up my work. It is too important, and there is still so much to be done."

"But I don't want you to give up your work!" George protested. "I think women should have the right to vote."

To prove his sincerity, George had his lawyer draw up a formal agreement. It stated that for two months every spring and every fall, Carrie would be free from all the duties of marriage. Also, she could travel whenever she needed to do so.

Carrie read the agreement and laughed happily. "Well, I guess you've convinced me," she said. "I'll be proud to marry you."

IN 1900, Susan B. Anthony resigned as president of the National Woman Suffrage Association. She was eighty years old. Who could take the place of such a revered leader? Why, Carrie Catt, of course.

In her inaugural speech, Carrie told her fellow members, "Our time has come. More women than ever are going to college. More women are taking jobs. We have plenty of enthusiastic young members. We must work harder than ever to achieve our goals."

Carrie urged local organizations to hold suffrage parades. In cities all over the country, women marched peacefully down the main streets. They carried banners that said, "Give us our rights. Let women vote."

Carrie also asked members to circulate petitions. "Ask everyone to sign them," she urged, "both men and women. Be polite, but firm."

I N 1918, the Nineteenth Amendment to the U.S. Constitution — the suffrage amendment — was put before the Congress once again. It had already been rejected by every Congress since 1878.

"The battle has begun," Carrie told her followers. "Two-thirds of both houses of Congress will have to approve the amendment. Then, 36 of the 48 states must ratify it before the first woman can cast her ballot."

Carrie had a secret goal that she didn't mention to anyone. "The amendment must pass in time for the 1920 Presidential election," she told herself. "That year will be the hundredth anniversary of Susan B. Anthony's birth. It would be a fitting tribute if women could vote in the election."

On January 10, 1918, Carrie stood in the visitor's gallery of the House of Representatives in Washington, D.C. She watched intently as the names of the members were called. One by one, the men called out their votes. The amendment had passed!

But the amendment faced stronger opposition in the Senate. Carrie encouraged her followers to continue their peaceful protests. She told them, "There is one thing mightier than kings or armies, congresses or political parties — the power of an idea when its time has come to move."

On June 4, 1919, the U.S. Senate passed the Nineteenth Amendment. By midnight the same day, Carrie had sent messages to her followers in each state. "You must keep the pressure on your governments," she told them. "Start letter-writing campaigns. Get the support of the well-known people in your state. Remember, our fate is in your hands."

Then Carrie sent telegrams to the state governors, asking them to call special sessions to vote on the amendment. Many did. In March 1920, Washington became the 35th state to ratify.

But which state would be the 36th? In August 1920, the governor of Tennessee called the state legislature into special session. Pro- and anti-suffragists poured into Nashville. Both sides gave roses to legislators who planned to vote in their favor. The pro-suffragists wore yellow roses. The anti-suffragists adopted the red rose as their symbol. The battle for suffrage became a "War of the Roses."

Carrie came to Nashville to lead the battle for ratification. She sent groups of local women to visit legislators who hadn't made up their minds. She toured the state, speaking at every opportunity. She and her followers were worried. The day was approaching, and they could count on only about half the votes — not a majority.

ON August 18, the morning of the vote, the capitol building was filled with people wearing red and yellow roses. One young legislator named Harry Burn had a red rose from the anti-suffragists pinned on his coat. But in his pocket was a letter from his mother. She had asked her son to vote for ratification.

The roll call began. Each of the legislators voted as expected, until Harry Burn's name was called. To everyone's surprise, he answered, "Aye!"

The suffragists held their breath as the roll call

continued. The vote stayed even. It was close, very close. When all the votes had been counted, the tally was 49-47. The amendment had been ratified! Burn had cast the tie-breaking vote! The suffragists leapt to their feet. They sang and wept and cheered.

Carrie was waiting a few blocks away in her hotel suite. She heard the commotion, and knew at once what it meant. "We have won!" she cried to her aides. "At last the battle is over!"

On the day of the 1920 Presidential election, Carrie stood at the ballot box. She was thinking of a little girl who had wanted to go into town with her father and vote. It had taken most of her life, but finally Carrie Chapman Catt could cast her first ballot. "This is for you, Aunt Susan," she thought as she dropped it into the box.

LANGSTON HUGHES

A BLACK POET SINGS AMERICA

My people are my life. I've known them and loved them in the Deep South, in Harlem, and in the heart of Africa. I try to write poems about their lives ... about their joys and hopes, about their sadness and anger and protest. As a black poet, I am their voice.

AN old woman with copper-colored skin and long, wavy black hair sat on the porch in her favorite rocking chair. Beside her sat her young grandson. She pulled an old shawl full of holes around her as she talked. The little boy was quiet. He liked listening to his grandmother's soft voice and the creaking of her rocker.

"One day," she said, "when I was a young wife, my husband rode out of town. Some friends of his told me that he had gone to join John Brown and his men. They were fighting against slavery. A few days after they raided Harper's Ferry, I received a package in the mail. It was my husband's shawl, full of bullet holes."

The old woman wasn't sad when she told this story. Instead she was proud. Her husband had died fighting for freedom.

"Later," she continued, "I married your grandfather. He also fought against slavery and discrimination. So did his brothers. Your great-uncle James was even a U.S. Congressman! So you see, Langston, you come from a proud family."

"Someday," Langston promised himself, "I will do something to make black people everywhere feel proud."

And that day seemed to come closer a few years later when Langston moved up North. His mother lived in Cleveland, Ohio, and he moved there to live with her. At Central High School, Langston was one of only a few blacks. But he got along well with the students. He was even elected class poet.

One day Langston was asked to read one of his poems before the school assembly. He stood nervously on the stage and looked out on a sea of white faces. "Relax," he told himself. "You are talking to your friends." He read his poem in a clear, steady voice. When he looked up, everyone was cheering. The applause felt good. "This is what I will do," thought Langston. "I will become a famous poet!"

LANGSTON had just graduated when he got a letter from his father. "Now that you have completed high school," it read, "come spend the summer at my home in Mexico."

Langston decided to go, and soon after he arrived, he wrote home to his mother: "You wouldn't believe how wealthy my father has become! He has a house in Mexico City and a ranch in the country. But I am ashamed of the way he treats his servants. All he cares about is making money, and he doesn't like poor people."

Langston's concern for his father's servants made him even more sure that he must devote his life to writing. But he knew he needed an education. Columbia University in New York was his choice. He hesitantly asked his father for help. To Langston's surprise, his father agreed.

"You will study business," his father said. "When you graduate, I will let you run my mines. You can live here in Mexico where black people have many opportunities. You'll earn plenty of money. You'll become a rich businessman!"

"But I want to be a writer," Langston protested. "I want to stay in the United States and make my living writing about black people."

His father laughed. "Who ever heard of a black writer? You'll never make any money."

"Some of my poems and essays have already been published in magazines," said Langston. "I'm sure I can do it!"

"I will pay for the first semester," said his father. "Then we shall see."

Langston began attending classes at Columbia University in 1921. But he was very disappointed. "This is wrong for me," he thought. "It has nothing to do with my life. But I *do* want to get my degree. Maybe I can stick it out."

But soon, Langston made a great discovery — Harlem! He loved the handsome buildings and the shady sidewalks. He also loved the jazz and blues played in Harlem's small cafes. Everywhere he looked, he saw black people laughing and enjoying themselves.

"At last," thought Langston, "I have found a place where I belong. Here I feel awake and alive!"

And Harlem was alive! In the early twenties, it was the capital of black America. Bessie Smith sang "the blues" for standing-room-only crowds. The streets were alive with the sound of great jazz performers. People flocked into the Harlem clubs. The music of Duke Ellington, King Oliver, and Louis Armstrong floated out into the night air. A whole nation was beginning to listen to the sounds of Harlem.

And writers flocked to Harlem, too. Many of them had read Langston's poems and shared their own poems and stories with him. Some of them would become famous: James Weldon Johnson, Claude McKay, and Countee Cullen. Never before had so much been written by black

writers or about black people. Pride and confidence shone in the words of these black writers.

Langston was filled with new energy. He wrote poems full of humor, poems that reflected the joys and optimism of the time. Life could be hard, but there would always be a place for laughter and for joy.

LIFE in Harlem led to a new curiosity. Langston wanted to learn more about his people and their African roots. He signed on as a crew member on a ship bound for Africa.

"At last," he told his mother, "I will see the land I have imagined since my childhood — the homeland of all black people."

But when the ship docked in Dakar, the poverty Langston saw around him made him sad. The beat and energy of Harlem seemed far away. He wrote a letter to one of his friends in New York. "Africa has been divided into colonies by the European countries. The black people have no say in their own governments. Everyone is very poor. Still, the land is beautiful and the people are very friendly. It is good to be among them."

Langston returned to the United States just in time to receive an invitation. A magazine in New York was having an awards dinner for black writers. Could he possibly attend?

Langston decided to go to the dinner. He wore his nicest suit, but he still felt uncomfortable. The room was crowded with people in crisp tuxedos and sparkling dresses. Langston fidgeted in his chair as the awards for poetry were announced. The speaker awarded the third prize, and then the second.

"And the first prize," he said, "goes to Langston Hughes!"

Langston had been chosen as the best black poet of 1925. He remembered what his friend from Harlem had once said: "Your poems speak for black people everywhere."

"I guess it's true!" Langston thought. "Now if I could only publish a book!"

As he stood thinking, a tall white man named Carl Van Vechten approached him.

"Congratulations!" he said. "I have read all of your work, and I think it is excellent. Would you mind if I showed some of your poems to my publisher? I think he might accept them."

Langston agreed. He returned to Washington, D.C., his new home. Then he received a letter from Van Vechten. His book would be published!

Langston was elated. But he began to worry. "Will anyone buy my book?" he wondered.

IN November 1925, Langston saw a notice in the newspaper. The famous poet, Vachel Lindsay, was going to give a reading at the hotel where Langston worked.

That evening, Langston saw Lindsay and his wife at a table in the dining room. This was his chance! Langston quickly wrote out three of his poems, and walked over to the table.

"I am an admirer of your work, Mr. Lindsay," he said. "Here are some poems I have written."

That night, at the poetry reading, Lindsay had a surprise for his audience.

"Tonight," he said, "I am going to read you someone else's poems."

He took Langston's poems from his pocket. He read:

When Susanna Jones wears red
Her face is like an ancient cameo
Turned brown by the ages.

When Susanna Jones wears red
A queen from some time-dead Egyptian night
Walks once again.

And the beauty of Susanna Jones in red
Burns in my heart a love-fire sharp like pain.

The audience was mesmerized. Lindsay read the other poems. When he was finished, the listeners applauded enthusiastically.

"These poems were written by a gifted young black man," Lindsay said. "In fact, he works in this very hotel!"

The next morning, reporters came to interview Langston. Newspapers across the country ran stories about the black busboy poet. Now everyone knew Langston's name.

IN January 1926, Langston received a copy of his newly published book, *The Weary Blues*. He held the volume in his hands, looking proudly at his name on the title page. "At last I am a real author," he thought. "This book will be in homes and libraries even after I am dead. People will read it and understand the beauty of black people."

Then Langston had a sad thought. "Many of the people I write for can't afford to buy books or even magazines. Somehow I must share my poetry with them. I must let them know I have written about their lives."

And so Langston began his travels around the country, reading his poems. The tour was a great success. He spoke wherever he could, at schools and churches. He looked into the faces of the people in the audience and felt happy. His poems were about their lives and their dreams.

Langston Hughes had kept the promise he made as a boy on his grandmother's porch. He had found a new way to make black people feel proud. His poems had given them a true voice ... a voice of spirit, dignity, and pride.

ALVIN YORK
THE RELUCTANT HERO

I'm not afraid. I believe in doing my duty. But I am against killing. I believe in God and the teachings of the Bible. And the Bible says, "Thou shalt not kill." So how can I go into the Army and kill people in a war? Tell me, what should I do?

ALVIN! Alvin York!" Rosier Pile called from the country road in front of a rustic wooden cabin near Pall Mall, Tennessee. "Alvin, here's some mail for you."

"Hi, Rosier!" replied York as he came out of the cabin. "What brings you to this neck of the woods?"

"I have some important mail for you. This is your draft notice. The Army wants you to help fight the war."

"The war? You mean the war overseas?" York asked. He knew that all of Europe had been fighting a war since 1914. During the last three years, thousands of people had been killed. In 1917, the United States agreed to enter the war to help England and France defeat Germany. The small U.S. Army needed more soldiers.

"But, Rosier, I can't fight in the war," explained York. "It's wrong to kill people."

"I know how you feel, Alvin," said Pile. "But the Army sure could use a strong young man like you. You're the best shot in the whole county. I've seen you shoot a turkey from 150 yards. And I don't believe you've ever missed a bull's-eye. You're a sure shot, all right."

"Shooting at targets and shooting at people are two different things," York said, shaking his head. "You know that I'm a faithful member of the church now. My life is different than it used to be. I've given up smoking, drinking, gambling, cussing, and brawling. I study the Bible every chance I get. And the Bible teaches that it's wrong to kill. I don't see how I can go fight."

"In that case," said Pile, "just say so. Put that on the registration form."

York took the form and scrawled across the back, "I don't want to fight. It's against the beliefs of my church."

York prayed that the Army would honor his wishes. Instead, the Army assigned him to a basic training camp near Atlanta, Georgia. He appealed again and again to be excused because of his religious beliefs. But he had no success. There seemed nothing he could do.

YORK braced himself for what was to come. On the day he left, he hugged his mother and his ten brothers and sisters. Then he caught a bus headed south, far from the green hills and farmland that he loved so dearly.

By the time he arrived in Atlanta, he was miserable. He missed his family already and worried about having to kill German soldiers. As soon as he settled in, he went to see his battalion commander, Major George E. Buxton, Jr.

"Sir," he said, "I try to live by the Bible. And the Bible says, 'Thou shalt not kill.'"

Major Buxton nodded. He, too, was a religious man. He understood Private York's concern.

"Yes," he said. "The Bible does say that. But the Bible also says, 'He that hath no sword, let him sell his cloak and buy one.' After all, you will not be killing for fun or profit. You will be fighting for a noble cause. You will be defending the lives of innocent people. You will be fighting for justice and freedom and democracy."

For almost two hours, York and Major Buxton talked about reasons for and against fighting in the war. Each tried to use passages from the Bible to prove his point. Major Buxton finally convinced York that his military service was a sacred duty. York promised to try to be a good soldier.

He impressed everyone with his shooting ability. He could hit the bull's-eye at any distance. But when the targets were dummies made to look like men, York wouldn't shoot. He still felt very strongly that killing was wrong. He went to see his commanding officer again. After more discussion, Major Buxton told him to take a ten-day leave.

"Go on home and think about it," the Major said. "If you really don't think you can be a soldier, I'll discharge you from the Army."

York thanked Major Buxton and headed back to Pall Mall. After greeting his family, he explained that he was going to spend time alone in the mountains trying to decide what to do. There among the stones and brush and fallen pine needles, he prayed for guidance. All night he stayed there, and he was there still when the sun rose the next morning. Finally, as a cool breeze began to stir the branches of the pine trees, York felt a sense of peace come over him.

"I know what to do now," he said. "As long as I do not forget God, my soul will be safe. I will go to Europe as a soldier. I will fight. I will do what must be done to serve my country."

ON October 7, 1918, York's battalion was in position along the top of a hill near the Argonne Forest in France. Ahead of them an open valley swept across to a row of hills. There, on the hilltops, sat German machine-gunners. These gunners controlled the railroad that supplied all the Germans in the Argonne Forest.

"We've got to take this forest out of German hands," Sergeant Bernard Early declared. "To do that, we must get rid of those machine-gunners and take control of the railroad."

York held his breath. He said a silent prayer that they would take the forest quickly.

"Then," he thought, "the killing will be over at last. We can return to a life of peace."

The next morning, York's platoon of seventeen soldiers was ordered to advance through the valley to scout the area. As soon as they began their march, the German gunners spotted them. The gunners launched a deadly barrage of bullets, and the Americans hit the ground. One tried to stand up again, but he was quickly shot down.

"This is a suicide mission!" shouted one soldier. "The German gunners can shoot us down like bowling pins!"

"Maybe," said Sergeant Early bravely, "but instead of lying here waiting for a bullet, let's cut to the left. We can swing wide and come up behind the Germans on that hill."

When Sergeant Early gave the word, York and the others made a mad dash to the left. They scrambled deep into the brush, then turned and headed forward. Slowly, carefully, they made their way behind enemy lines.

SUDDENLY they spotted a small hut in a clearing. Next to the hut sat two dozen German soldiers, casually eating their breakfast.

"We've found the headquarters for the German machine-gunners," hissed Sergeant Early. "Look — up there on the hill — you can see the gunners who are on duty!"

York followed Sergeant Early's gaze.

"Sure enough," he whispered.

He and the others were only fifty yards from the top of the hill. He could see the gunners, their backs turned, firing at the American troops across the valley.

"Okay, let's go!" commanded Sergeant Early. He fired his rifle at one of the soldiers near the hut and ran forward. York and the others followed.

The Germans around the hut surrendered without a fight. But as the Americans lined up the prisoners, the gunners on the hill heard the commotion. They swiveled their guns away from the valley and took aim at the clearing.

"Look out!" yelled York.

But it was too late. Sergeant Early fell to the ground, mortally wounded. Eight other Americans also fell. Instantly the other men ran into the woods. But York crouched where he was. He showed no fear of the German gunners.

The gunners were having to shoot high to avoid hitting the captured soldiers. As the bullets whizzed all around York, he steadied his rifle and took aim. One by one, he shot at the gunners on the hill. And one by one, they fell.

Then York saw six Germans rushing down the hill at him. His rifle clip was empty, so he picked up an automatic pistol dropped by one of the captured Germans.

"Keep calm," he told himself. "Just keep calm and imagine you're back home on a wild turkey shoot."

York squeezed the trigger six times. All six of the Germans fell. Then York called to the remaining gunners to surrender.

Shaken by the death of so many of their comrades, the gunners obeyed. Meekly they raised their hands in the air.

York and the few soldiers left in his platoon rounded up a total of 132 prisoners and marched them out of the forest back to American lines.

"I can't believe it!" cried one stunned officer who saw them coming. "Alvin York has captured the whole German army!"

YORK had not captured the entire army. But his actions did allow the Americans to capture the railroad lines. That led to the German defeat at the Argonne Forest and, a few months later, to the end of the war.

York was greeted with honors when he returned to the United States. He received the Congressional Medal of Honor for his actions. He was the single biggest hero of the war. He did not want to be a celebrity, though.

"I'm really no hero," he told reporters as he headed back home to Pall Mall. "I just did what had to be done."

Despite his modesty, Alvin York *was* a hero. His skill and bravery helped end the war and saved countless lives. This country boy had risked his life to help bring peace back to the world.

RUDOLPH VALENTINO

THE KING OF HEARTS

I love to perform! I've already become the King of the Tango at Maxim's. People come here every night just to watch me dance. But the movies! People are flocking to them, waiting in line for hours. I know that I could become a success on film. Maybe someday I'll be famous throughout the country!

RUDOLPH Valentino sat nervously in June Mathis's outer office, wringing his hands.

"What if she doesn't like me?" Valentino whispered to his friend Norman Kerry.

"Don't worry, Rudy. Just be yourself. She'll love you," Kerry reassured him.

At last Miss Mathis summoned Valentino into her office. There she introduced him to Rex Ingram, a movie director, and invited him to sit down. He sank into a velvet-covered chair and crossed his legs awkwardly.

"Mr. Valentino, as you know, we are in the process of choosing a male lead for Metro's new movie, *The Four Horsemen of the Apocalypse*." June Mathis paused. "Why don't you tell us a little bit about yourself?"

Valentino took a deep breath and began hesitantly. "I come from a little town in Italy. As a boy, I loved to wander through the olive orchards and pretend to be a brave explorer or a mighty king." Valentino's dark eyes brightened as he remembered those happy days.

"When I was eleven, my father died. I moved with my brother to the city. As I grew older, I began to like the girls." Valentino gave a happy laugh and shook his head. "I was always getting into trouble because of the girls."

"But I knew Italy held no future for me. I was restless. I craved excitement and travel," he said, gesturing passionately. "I heard so many wonderful things about the United States. I knew that if I came to America, I could make my fortune. But it has been more difficult than I expected. For a while I was a gardener, then a dancer ..." Valentino's voice drifted off as he recalled his disappointments. "But I have always wanted to be an actor more than anything in the world!" He peered intently into Miss Mathis's eyes. "It is my dream to be a movie star!"

Miss Mathis was entranced by his look, his face, his eyes. She returned his gaze, feeling herself drawn deeper and deeper under his spell.

Rex Ingram spoke up, "Yes, every actor wants to be a star."

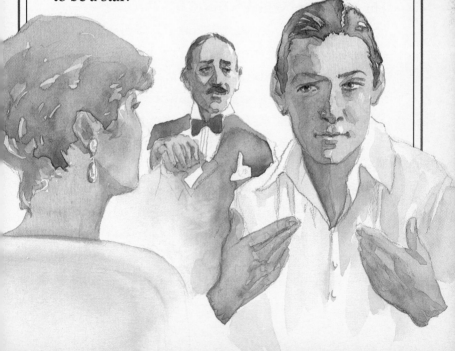

Miss Mathis blinked, trying to focus on her job and draw herself away from Valentino's magnetic presence.

"Well, thank you, Mr. Valentino," she stammered. "Thank you for your time. You will be hearing from us shortly."

She shook his hand and ushered him out of her office.

OUTSIDE, Valentino collapsed into an anxious heap. "I don't think they liked me," he moaned. "We didn't even talk about the part!"

Even as Kerry tried to comfort him, June Mathis was raving about him to Rex Ingram.

"He's perfect!" she declared enthusiastically. "Rudolph Valentino is just the man to play Julio."

"Are you joking?" cried Ingram. "He's too soft! He's too limp! Where's the flair?"

June Mathis shook her head. "I'm sure I'm right," she said firmly. "He may be unpolished. But he has the makings of a star. I could feel it. There's something very romantic about him — and his eyes just make you want to melt."

Ingram threw up his hands. "It's your decision," he said.

When Valentino learned that he had won the part, he was thrilled. The sudden success affirmed his faith in himself. He arrived on the movie set, glowing with confidence. From the moment he shot the first scene, he captured the hearts of the crew and cast. Even Ingram had to admit that Valentino was perfect for the film.

"His eyes seem to look right through the camera," Ingram marveled. "And his movements are so dramatic."

The Four Horsemen of the Apocalypse was released in 1921. Overnight Rudolph Valentino became the nation's first major movie idol. Women, especially, flocked to theaters to see him. They screamed whenever he appeared on the screen. They moaned when his eyes flashed intently. And many of them fainted when he struck his final, heroic pose.

"Audiences are going crazy!" Ingram told June Mathis in delight. "That movie has grossed over four million dollars! It's the most popular movie ever!"

"Yes," smiled Miss Mathis. "And it's all because of Rudolph Valentino."

VALENTINO loved his newfound fame. He pranced around the streets of Hollywood wearing expensive clothing and gold jewelry. He spent money as fast as he earned it.

"At first I was a bit bewildered by the public's love for me," he confided to Kerry. "But now I think I understand. I am a great artist. Perhaps the greatest actor who has ever lived!"

Kerry looked at Valentino solemnly. "Confidence is a good thing, Rudy," he said. "But don't take this too seriously. Remember, the American people are a little wild right now. The war is over, and good times are here. The 1920's economy is booming. People are dizzy with good fortune. You see it everywhere. They're dancing new dances like the Charleston and partying all the time. Why, they're even having contests to see who can sit up on a flagpole the longest."

"I do not see your point," Valentino said coldly.

"My point, Rudy, is that the world is crazy right now. And you shouldn't believe everything people say."

"But the people are right," Valentino insisted. "They say I am a genius, and I am."

Kerry did not respond. But the next time he tried to visit Valentino at home, he was not permitted to enter. The butler brought him a short note from Valentino. It read: "Anyone who is not committed to me and does not believe in my talent is not welcome here."

After cutting his ties with Kerry, Valentino found new friends who told him what he wanted to hear. He surrounded himself with people who lavished praise on him. As they fed his ego, he demanded more money from the movie studio.

When Metro refused to meet his demands, he moved to Paramount. There his salary steadily climbed from $400 a week to over $1,200 a week.

Paramount first starred him in *The Sheik*, in which he played an Arab kidnapper who falls in love with his female hostage. Valentino cast many smoldering glances at his leading lady and left the audience mesmerized.

Moviegoers loved the film. Some people even began decorating their homes in Arabian styles. Thousands of adoring women swooned whenever Valentino's name was mentioned. People imitated his dress, gestures, and lifestyle.

IN July 1926, Paramount released a new film, *The Son of the Sheik*.

"When the movie opens in New York, I am going to make a personal appearance," Valentino told the executives at Paramount. "My fans deserve to see me in person."

Valentino traveled to New York to attend the opening of *The Son of the Sheik*. But although he loved the attention of his fans, this time they overwhelmed him. Desperate to see their idol, they crowded around him, screaming and shouting. They tore at his clothes, his hands, his hair. Frantic for a souvenir, one woman even ripped the pockets off his coat. Another stole his hat. One woman tackled him and tried to take his shoe-laces. Luckily, the police stepped in to rescue Valentino from his fans.

On August 15, 1926, a month after the release of *The Son of the Sheik*, Valentino unexpectedly collapsed in his hotel room. The 31-year-old king of the cinema was rushed to a New York hospital.

Doctors soon diagnosed the trouble — appendicitis. They operated, and Valentino seemed to be recovering. But on August 23, his lungs collapsed. Valentino was dead.

When the news spread, fans were overcome with grief. They could not believe that their beloved Valentino was gone.

ACROSS the country, people shed tears of mourning for their great idol. And in New York, where the Campbell Funeral Home held the star's body, a riot broke out.

"I've got to see him!" shouted one frenzied fan.

"You must let us in! We must say good-bye to Rudolph!" cried another.

The director of the funeral home agreed to let the public view the body. Soon the line of mourners stretched for almost a mile. At first everything went peacefully. But then a rumor spread through the crowd that the funeral home would not be opened after all. Hysterical people stormed the building, desperate to see Valentino's body. They crashed through a plate glass window, trampled each other, and hit police officers. Many of the rioters were sobbing as they lashed out. "I will die if you don't let me see him!" shouted one young woman.

The riot lasted all day. By the time the police

gained control, dozens of people had been injured. Many ended up in the hospital. The scene repeated itself the next day. Police again found themselves battling a huge mob of crazed mourners. Finally the Campbell Funeral Home stopped all public viewing of the body.

Even after the rioting ended, the country remained in shock. For two solid weeks, Rudolph Valentino's name appeared in every newspaper headline. His name was on everyone's lips. Theaters ran extra showings of *The Son of the Sheik,* and the movie broke all box office records.

Valentino's sudden death crystallized the fame of this first movie idol. His passionate eyes and magnetic personality were burned forever into his fans' memory. Even today his name, more than any other, brings forth images of grace, romance, and passion.

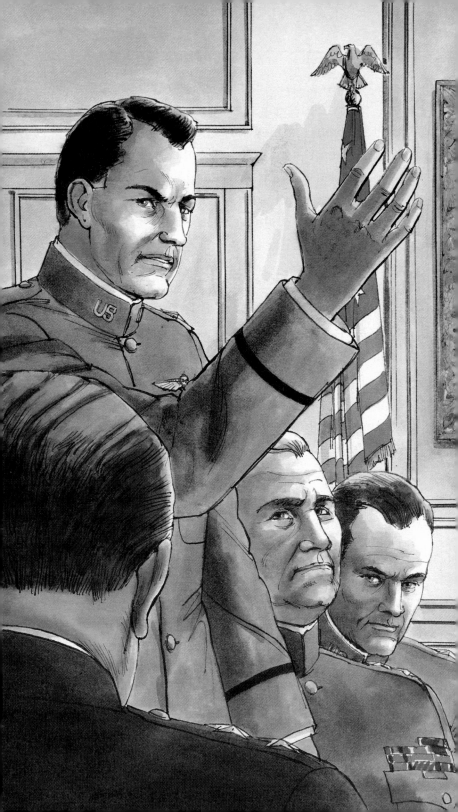

BILLY MITCHELL
CRUSADER FOR AIR POWER

Don't you generals see? The world is changing. You're still fighting the last war. You're thinking in terms of foot soldiers and cavalry. The airplane has changed all that! In the future, wars will be won or lost in the air! We must establish an air force!

U.S. ARMY General Billy Mitchell stood ready to face a congressional committee in Washington, D.C.

"Well, today is the day," he said to himself. "Today I'm about to say what needs to be said!"

It was February 3, 1920. All eyes turned toward Billy as he took the stand and began to speak.

"America is in great danger," he proclaimed. "In the past, we depended on the Army and Navy. But these two departments can no longer protect us. Something else is needed." He paused dramatically.

"We need a strong, independent *air force*. We need fleets of planes and trained pilots. During battle, planes can move quickly toward and away from the enemy. They can speed to a target, carry out their mission, and return before the enemy can counterattack. Foot soldiers, tanks, and battleships served us well in the past. But they are no longer enough."

Secretary of the Navy Josephus Daniels stared icily at Mitchell. Mitchell returned his stare. He knew that the military leaders didn't like the idea of an air force. They didn't want to share their power with a new department. Besides, they had no faith in airplanes.

Mitchell pressed on, in spite of the chill in the

room. "Planes are not expensive to build. We could build a thousand bombers for the cost of a single battleship."

The Secretary of the Navy burst out laughing. "Your statements are absurd!" he shouted. "Airplanes are nothing more than novelties. They will never be an important part of any country's system of defense."

"That's not true!" retorted Mitchell. "Other countries are already building military planes. These planes will be able to destroy military *and* industrial centers from the air. The Army and Navy will not be able to fight back!"

As Mitchell left the committee meeting, he heard Secretary Daniels and the other officers chuckling.

"Let them laugh," Mitchell thought with contempt. "They'll see."

A YEAR later Mitchell was asked to testify again before a congressional committee. He pleaded earnestly for an independent air force. Then, without warning, he issued a stunning challenge.

"Military planes can destroy and sink any ship in existence!" he declared. "And I can prove it. In fact, I propose a test: let the Navy set up an old battleship off the coast. Then let me send bomber pilots up to attack it. That will show you how effective air power can be!"

The committee members were shocked. Then their shock turned to excitement. This would be the perfect way to test Mitchell's claims.

Secretary Daniels scoffed when he heard Mitchell's proposal. "Airplanes don't have the accuracy to bomb a warship!" he jeered. "Even if the bombs do hit a ship, they won't hurt it! Those ships are indestructible."

Nevertheless, on July 21, 1921, Secretary Daniels positioned an old German battleship off the coast of Virginia. Mitchell ordered his bombers to attack it. At first the planes pelted the ship with small bombs, barely making a dent in the "unsinkable" vessel. Then Mitchell ordered a 2,000-pound bomb dropped. With a flip of the

lever, the pilot scored a direct hit. The old battleship sank to the bottom of the sea.

Across the country people were in shock.
Newspapers ran photographs of the attack on the
ship. As word of Mitchell's success spread, he
became a national hero. People became more
aware of the need for air power, and they rallied
in support of Mitchell's call for a U.S. Air Force.

Back in Washington, however, Army and Navy
officials were furious.

"Let's get rid of this man," stormed Secretary Daniels. "He's a troublemaker — where can we send him?"

"How about Asia?" suggested an aide. "He could scout out the military forces of China and Japan."

Before he knew it, Billy was on his way to Asia. But he was not discouraged. "This will give me a chance to see if the Asian countries are developing air power," he thought. "I'll make myself useful as an observer."

MITCHELL began to discover some disturbing things. Japan had amassed a large number of military planes. The country was building more planes each day. Surely this was cause for alarm! Billy returned to America in 1924 and reported the news to a special congressional committee.

"Without an air force, we cannot protect ourselves from attack. The Japanese are building up their air force. The only way to scare them off is to have strong air power of our own."

"Don't be ridiculous," snapped one Congressman. "Japan is nothing to worry about. Besides, air power is not the way to keep this country safe."

Mitchell threw up his hands in dismay. He went to see his superior officer, Major General M. M. Patrick. In the general's office, he launched into his familiar pitch for a separate air force.

General Patrick didn't want to hear it. He asked Mitchell to drop the subject, but Mitchell persisted. Finally, General Patrick lost his temper.

"Billy," he said, "I'm beginning to think that you're nothing but a nuisance. And this army has no room for fellows like you."

"But, sir ..." Mitchell protested.

"In fact," continued Patrick, "I am going to recommend that you be removed as Assistant Chief of Air Service."

Mitchell stood in silent shock. He had devoted his career to advancing air power. He couldn't believe that his job might now be taken away from him. Mitchell argued with General Patrick, but the general would not change his position.

In the spring of 1925, Mitchell was officially dropped to the rank of colonel and given an unimportant assignment in San Antonio, Texas.

Mitchell might have settled into a quiet life at the San Antonio base, but two things happened that he could not ignore.

In early September, a tragic report came from Honolulu, Hawaii. A naval plane had been lost at sea. The pilot had sent several emergency messages, but naval air controllers lost contact with him. Two days later, a second tragedy occurred. A Navy air blimp ran into a thunderstorm in the Ohio River Valley. The storm wrecked the blimp and killed fourteen crew members.

"That proves my point!" declared Mitchell.

From his home in San Antonio, Mitchell wrote an explosive press statement. In it he said: "The Navy knows nothing about air safety! None of the naval leaders have ever flown a plane. They know nothing about aviation! The Navy simply should not be in charge of the military's air service."

Mitchell blamed the War Department for the deaths of innocent men. "The leaders in the War Department are incompetent!" he wrote. "They have neglected their duties to these airmen. The actions of the War Department and Navy border on treason!"

After writing the statement, Mitchell sent it to local and national newspapers.

"I know this will ruin my career," he thought. "But I must speak out. I must speak the truth as I see it."

MITCHELL knew that the War Department would never forgive him for his statement. As he expected, he was soon relieved of all military duties. He was ordered to appear before a military court for a trial. He was charged with breaking military rules of discipline and defiance of his superior officers. On October 25, 1925, Billy Mitchell appeared in court.

Mitchell pleaded his case with passion and dignity, expressing his belief that America needed a strong air defense. He explained that since the military leaders wouldn't listen to him, he had resorted to public statements.

"The Army and Navy have betrayed the trust of the American people," he said. "We trust these departments to provide adequate defenses, and they aren't doing that."

For seven weeks the military court listened to the evidence. Although Mitchell won the support of the American people, he lost his case. On December 17, 1925, he was found guilty. He was sentenced to a five-year suspension without pay.

Mitchell was both angry and bitter about his treatment by the military. In February 1926, he resigned from the Army rather than accept the suspension. But he never gave up his fight for an independent air force. For the next ten years, until his death at age 56, he continued to warn Americans about the need for an air force.

"Without air defenses, we are an easy target. Japanese bombers might come out of the sky at any moment. They could drop bombs that would wipe out the naval base in Hawaii. I can almost see them now — flying out of the morning sun in a V formation!"

N O ONE in power paid any attention to Mitchell's warning. But a few years after his death, his words came back to haunt all Americans. On December 7, 1941, the Japanese staged a surprise attack on the U.S. naval base in Hawaii. At 7:55 that morning, they began a deadly attack on Pearl Harbor, flying out of the sky in V formations. The attack destroyed the U.S. Navy battleships in the Pacific fleet and brought America into World War II.

Billy Mitchell had been right.

Finally, in 1947, the United States Air Force was created as a separate department. Today more than 600,000 men and women actively serve in its ranks. The Air Force holds a position of equal importance with the Army and Navy in the system of defense. Although it took many years, Billy Mitchell's dream finally came true.

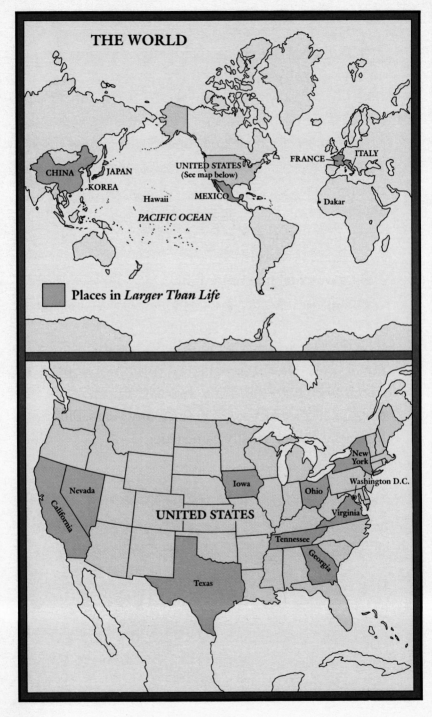